The 60-Minute Active Training Series

HOW TO ENCOURAGE CONSTRUCTIVE FEEDBACK FROM OTHERS

T0327751

PARTICIPANT'S WORKBOOK

Mel Silberman and Freda Hansburg

Copyright © 2005 by John Wiley & Sons, Inc.

Published by Pfeiffer
An Imprint of Wiley
989 Market Street, San Francisco, CA 94103-1741   www.pfeiffer.com

For additional copies/bulk purchases of this book in the U.S. please contact 800-274-4434.

Pfeiffer books and products are available through most bookstores. To contact Pfeiffer directly call our Customer Care Department within the U.S. at 800-274-4434, outside the U.S. at 317-572-3985 or fax 317-572-4002 or www.pfeiffer.com.

Pfeiffer also publishes its books in a variety of electronic formats. Some content that appears in print may not be available in electronic books.

ISBN: 0-7879-7352-1

Acquiring Editor: Martin Delahoussaye   Senior Production Editor: Dawn Kilgore

Director of Development: Kathleen Dolan Davies   Manufacturing Supervisor: Becky Carreno

Developmental Editor: Susan Rachmeler   Interior Design: Erin Zeltner

Editor: Rebecca Taff

Printed in the United States of America

Printing 10   9   8   7   6   5   4   3   2   1

CONTENTS

About This Brief Training Session 1

How Many Squares? 2

Self-Assessment 3

Animal Feedback 4

Why People Withhold Feedback 5

Ways to Encourage Feedback from Others 6

Requesting Feedback 7

Try It: Experiments in Change 8

Reading 9

While it's been said that "feedback is the breakfast of champions," most people skip the meal. Everyone wants to receive feedback, but virtually no one takes the risk to give it.

Feedback is often withheld because a person is not sure the potential receiver wants or would appreciate the feedback. In addition, a person may feel that he or she is overstepping the bounds, especially if the receiver is a colleague or boss. Or perhaps the receiver would become angry, or even seek reprisal. Finally, the person may just not want the hassle.

Because feedback on the job can be a scarce commodity, "people smart" individuals understand that waiting for feedback from others isn't enough. Instead, they practice the strategy of inviting feedback from a wide circle of people. To motivate these people to give them useful feedback, they also know several ways to *encourage* honest and constructive information.

This training session provides the strategies that you can use to encourage people at work to exchange honest, constructive feedback. It will be especially useful for you if you are willing to take responsibility for your own growth and development . . . regardless of your job or role.

You will have the opportunity:

- To discuss the reasons why people withhold feedback

- To learn ways to encourage honest, constructive feedback from others

- To identify the kinds of feedback you really want to receive

- To select "experiments in change" at work

How many squares do you see in the following grid?

My answer is: ___

How would you rate your ability to seek feedback from others?

4 = consistently   3 = often   2 = sometimes   1 = never

___ 1. I am open to feedback about my performance.

___ 2. I seek feedback from a wide range of people.

___ 3. I listen to feedback I receive from others.

___ 4. I seek feedback to improve myself . . . not to fish for compliments.

___ 5. I thank people for giving me feedback, whether it's helpful or not.

Instructions: From the list below, select the animal that most resembles your partner, considering both physical characteristics and personal qualities. Please make your selection even if you have no prior familiarity with your partner.

DO NOT TELL YOUR PARTNER YOUR SELECTION UNTIL TOLD TO DO SO. THINK ABOUT HOW YOU WILL EXPLAIN YOUR CHOICE TO YOUR PARTNER.

LION	SQUIRREL
MONKEY	DOLPHIN
TIGER	GIRAFFE
KANGAROO	HORSE
BIRD (specify type)	BEAR (specify type)
CAT (specify type)	DOG (specify type)

WHY PEOPLE WITHHOLD FEEDBACK

Think about your own situation at work and decide which of the following are reasons why people do not give you feedback. Make notes if desired.

1. I don't ask them for feedback.

2. I am not specific about the feedback I want.

3. I don't give them time to think about what feedback to give me.

4. I don't assure them that it is safe to be honest.

5. I don't let them know how much I sincerely value their input.

WAYS TO ENCOURAGE FEEDBACK FROM OTHERS

Read the following and decide which ways of encouraging feedback could work for you. Make notes of situations in which you could use any of the methods.

1. Present a sincere rationale for wanting their feedback.

   "I'm serious about improving my meeting facilitation skills, and you could really help me by sharing some of your thoughts about how I led our last meeting."

2. Be specific about the feedback you're seeking.

   "Would you please tell me when you notice me interrupting others?"

3. Give others time to prepare their feedback.

   "I'd really like your feedback about how I handled this presentation. Would you be willing to get back to me by the end of the week with your thoughts?"

4. Self-assess to start the process.

   "I thought I was pretty patient with Ron's objections, but I'm not sure I did a very good job supporting your views. What did you think?"

5. Make the feedback anonymous.

   "I'm asking several people for feedback on my performance as a computer consultant. Please respond to the questions below and return it my mailbox anonymously."

6. Ask for suggestions only.

   "What do you think I could have done differently to try to close that sale?"

List below the names of people with whom you work:

_____   _____   _____

_____   _____   _____

_____   _____   _____

Select someone from whom you would like to receive feedback and specify what you want feedback about from that person:

_____

_____

_____

What strategies will you use to encourage feedback from that person?

❑ 1. Present a sincere rationale for wanting his/her feedback.

❑ 2. Be specific about the feedback I'm seeking.

❑ 3. Give that person time to prepare the feedback.

❑ 4. Self-assess to start the process.

❑ 5. Make the feedback anonymous.

❑ 6. Ask for suggestions only.

Select one these "experiments in change" to do within the next week.

❑ *Requesting Feedback*

Identify someone from whom you'd like to receive feedback. Approach the person and say, *"I'd like to improve my [select a quality, skill, or behavior]. Could you tell me how well I'm doing right now, and also let me know in the future if there's any change for the better or worse? Could we set a time to do this?"* Evaluate the results.

❑ *Going Beyond Performance Appraisals*

Think about the last performance appraisal you received. Well before the next one is scheduled, identify areas for improvement that were identified in your last performance appraisal and your manager's opinions about the progress you've shown. Make it easy for him or her by posing specific questions or even asking for unofficial ratings of your current performance.

❑ *Approaching Someone Who Is Afraid to Give Feedback*

Think of someone you know who, in your opinion, would be very nervous about giving you feedback. Approach the person and explain how you see your own performance in an area that needs improvement. Critique your own behavior and then ask the person if he or she agrees with you. Evaluate the results.

ENCOURAGING HONEST, CONSTRUCTIVE FEEDBACK

Reading

Consider each of the following hypothetical work situations. Would you want others to tell you if the situation were true of you? Would you be likely to tell someone else if the situation were true of him or her?

- Giving a presentation with a piece of spinach stuck between your teeth

- Writing poor quality business letters

- Not appearing as energetic as you used to

- Mispronouncing a customer's name

- Having a habit that distracts colleagues in meetings, such as jingling coins in your pocket or tapping with your pen

- Dressing inappropriately for the office

Although you probably wouldn't be happy to learn that any of these scenarios applied to you, if you are like most people, you would be more willing to *receive* such feedback (assuming it were true) than to *volunteer* it to someone else. This is the basic feedback dilemma: We all have blind spots and need others to reveal them to us, but others are often reluctant to do so.

Think of all the reasons you might hesitate to tell a colleague (or worse, your boss) that he or she was guilty of any of these faux pas. Perhaps you're not sure the person would appreciate the feedback. Maybe you would be overstepping your bounds, especially if the person is your boss. Maybe he or she would become angry, or even seek reprisal. Perhaps you just don't want the hassle.

Because honest feedback on the job is an important and scarce commodity, "people smart" individuals have learned that waiting for it isn't enough. Instead, they practice the strategy of inviting feedback from a wide circle of people. Even when they disagree with the feedback they receive, these individuals know that they are better off knowing how others see them than they are guessing.

Many companies have policies mandating 360-degree feedback (that is, feedback from supervisors, peers, and direct reports), often in the form of surveys completed annually or quarterly. Although this is clearly a step in the right direction, savvy individuals don't just rely on a formal policy. They also take the initiative to seek out ongoing "feedback relationships" with others in their work lives.

In a feedback relationship, there is a shared commitment to exchange perspectives about one another's performance and about the relationship. Both parties feel free to offer and request input from one another. Imagine having genuine, spontaneous 360-degree feedback relationships at work. Consider what some of the benefits might be:

- Not having to guess what others really think about your work

- Obtaining a wide enough sample of opinion to recognize trends (as well as input that's off the wall)

- Learning who tends to give the most helpful feedback on specific issues, so that you know whom to approach about what

- Hearing more praise than you are accustomed to receiving

- Receiving more ideas and suggestions to help you improve

- Feeling closer to the people you work with

- Getting some things off your chest instead of keeping them to yourself

Most of us don't experience consistent feedback relationships on the job. And yet, all of that information is out there, just waiting to be harvested—if we can learn how to ask for it convincingly. Unfortunately, feedback requests often come across as superficial, or worse, as fishing for compliments. Consider this exchange between Alan, who has just concluded a presentation to his clients, and Paige, his assistant:

Alan: *"How was the presentation?"*
Paige (hesitates): *"You did . . . great."*
Alan: *"Paige, you seem a little hesitant. Are you sure I didn't bore them?"*
Paige (trying to sound convincing): *"No, honestly, you were really great. I think they loved it."*
Alan: *"Good, I thought I nailed it!"*

Afraid to give Alan any criticism, Paige withholds her true opinions and offers him bland reassurances, which Alan is only too eager to embrace. But what if the clients didn't think much of his presentation either? By missing out on constructive feedback, Alan loses an opportunity to correct course. Consider how Paige might have responded if Alan's feedback request had sounded like this:

"Paige, I'm concerned about the future of this account, because I'm picking up signals that they're not fully happy with our services. I would really appreciate your honest impressions of how that presentation went. In particular, I'd like to hear how you think I handled their questions at the end because, frankly, I'm not sure I really understood their concerns. If you'd rather not just answer off the top of your head, how about giving it some thought and getting back to me with your feedback later today?"

Better, right? Let's zero in on the success strategies that make this a more "people smart" feedback invitation.

Four Ways to Encourage Feedback

Here are four S's (that's "S" as in "success") to keep in mind when you are seeking quality feedback from others. Incorporate these elements in order to reduce people's discomfort and improve the chances of getting their honest and constructive input.

1. *Sincerity.* Present an authentic rationale for wanting someone's feedback.

   - *"I'm serious about improving my meeting facilitation skills and you could really help me by sharing some of your thoughts about how I led the meeting we just had."*

   - *"You have a lot of experience with this equipment and I'm new at this. Would you be willing to watch me while I try to operate it and tell me how I'm doing?"*

2. *Specificity.* Be clear about the particular feedback you are seeking.

   - *"Would you please tell me when you notice me interrupting others?"*

   - *"What do you think I could have done differently to try to handle that customer?"*

3. *Safety.* Avoid putting others on the spot when you ask them for feedback. In fact, go the extra mile to make them comfortable. Sometimes it helps to change the scene and talk over a lunch table instead of a conference table. Give others time to prepare their feedback, or even offer anonymity when appropriate.

   - *"I'd really like your feedback about how I handled this presentation. Would you be willing to get back to me later this week with your thoughts?"*

   - *"When we meet with Lucy this afternoon, would you please observe how well I do at dealing with her anxieties and give me your comments and suggestions afterwards?"*

4. *Self-critique.* Start the process by acknowledging some of your own flaws as a way to model and give permission for honest feedback.

   - *"I thought I was pretty patient with Ron's objections, but I'm not sure I did a very good job supporting our views. What did you think?"*

   - *"I feel like I'm getting more comfortable with these cold calls, but I wonder if I could do better at closing the sale."*

The Power of Positive Feedback

Whether or not you agree with the feedback others give in response to your requests, be sure to thank them for being willing to share it with you. You may have heard the adage "Feedback is a gift." Bear in mind that it is also a gift you can "return to the store" if it just doesn't fit.

A concern that people in organizations frequently raise is the difficulty of getting positive feedback from supervisors. Too often, managers adopt an attitude of "no news is good news," expecting silence to be interpreted as satisfaction. We've even heard the explicit view that "professionals shouldn't need to be praised for doing a good job."

We think this is misguided.

For years, psychologists have known that reward is a more powerful tool than punishment when the goal is to shape behavior. Teachers have a saying, "Catch 'em doing something right," that applies the same principle. Positive feedback isn't just a way to make people feel good: it's a powerful motivator. When you pinpoint something an individual has done well and ask for more of the same, you are providing valuable information. Withhold the feedback and you waste an opportunity.

Can you request positive feedback from your boss without sounding needy? We think so. One way to do this is to use the teacher trick and capitalize on the situation if your boss *does* happen to volunteer a compliment. Thank him or her and add: *"Your feedback means a lot to me. I find I learn even more when you point out what I'm doing that's on target. I hope you won't mind if I ask you to share more of those reactions in the future."* Among the four S's, sincerity is probably key in requesting positive feedback from above. Help your boss recognize that you're not just fishing for compliments, but seeking to fine-tune your performance when you solicit his or her feedback.

When It's Your Turn to Give Feedback

Savvy individuals also know how to give feedback in a sensitive and skillful way. If you think about it, being a frequent feedback recipient attunes you to how it feels to be on the receiving end and helps you become more conscious of how your own feedback may be experienced by others. It's better to offer feedback provisionally than as a pronouncement. Let your words and tone convey that, after all, it's an opinion you are sharing, rather than one of the ten commandments. When they have occasion to share feedback, here are the strategies that "people smart" individuals practice. You don't have to use all of them, but consider which ones you might want to practice more:

Ask Permission.   Before plunging ahead, check to see whether the other person is ready and willing to hear you out.

- *"Is this a good time for me to tell you some thoughts I have about. . . ?"*

- *"Would you be open to hearing some feedback about . . . ?"*

Compliment First.   Start by reflecting something you genuinely value or appreciate about the person—especially something relevant to the subject of your feedback.

- *"You have a warm, friendly tone with the customers you call."*

- *"You obviously did your homework. You had plenty of facts to back up your project status report."*

Focus on Behavior.   Describe specific actions, rather than labeling the person. Give examples when possible.

- *"It seems to me that you tend to focus on the negatives rather than the positive when you conduct performance appraisals. For instance, just now, you told Mr. Jones. . . ."*

- *"There were a couple of times when, in your eagerness to share your data, you may have misunderstood the client's question. Remember when Claire asked about. . . ?"*

Offer Suggestions.   Give one or two concrete recommendations for improvement. This way you are focusing on the future, not the past. Make sure your suggestions are doable for the person.

- *"Perhaps before making sales calls you could write up a little crib sheet to remind yourself of possible benefits you can mention."*

- *"If you paraphrase the question before you start to answer it, you can check whether you have a handle on the person's real concern."*

Ask for Reactions.   Check to see whether the person understands and/or agrees with your feedback. Correct any misimpressions she or he may have received.

- *"Do you feel that this is true?"*

- *"Is this helpful?"*

- *"How do you see it?"*

- *"Is that okay with you?"*

When you take the time to give feedback in a careful and caring way, others are more likely to listen and consider what you say to them. They may also be more likely to make an effort to give you quality feedback in return.

Three Challenging Situations

Below are three situations that may have occurred in your own work. Read the question posed in each situation and see what an effective solution looks like.

Situation 1
"My boss doesn't believe in giving praise. Her attitude is that if she doesn't complain about my work, I should know she's satisfied. But I feel a need for more specific feedback about what I'm doing right. How can I convey this to her without sounding needy?"

The key to persuading your boss to give you more positive feedback lies in the rationale you give for your request. Give her a genuine reason why you want her feedback. *Don't say (or convey): "I want your feedback because my pitiful, shriveled ego is starving for praise."* Instead present a sincere reason that includes a benefit to her or to the organization. Here are some examples:

- *"You may not realize how helpful your feedback is to me. Even when I do something well, I don't always understand exactly what was right about it. When you clarify this for me, it takes away the guesswork and helps me to be more consistent in my performance."*

- *"I'd like to build on my strengths. You usually have excellent suggestions about how I can apply my successes to new areas. Maybe I could take on some new projects and reduce some of the load on others."*

- *"Sometimes I'm pretty hard on myself. If I know you're happy with the work I'm producing, I'll be less likely to waste my energy worrying about it and I'll probably be more productive."*

If your boss still resists, don't become defensive. Calmly reiterate your request and look for a way to "get your foot in the door" without expecting your boss to make a total or permanent commitment. Perhaps your boss would agree to share some positive feedback about a specific project you completed, or for a trial period of a few weeks. Maybe she would be willing to email some favorable comments to you if she doesn't have time to meet in person. If she resists even these small steps, you might say: *"I understand that my request is inconvenient for you, but it's really important to me. I hope you'll at least agree to give it some further thought."*

Situation 2

"Sometimes it seems like the more work I put in, the less I get back from my teammates. When I most want and need constructive feedback I'm usually disappointed at how little they offer or how off the wall the feedback I do get from them is. How can I coax some useful feedback out of them?"

There are many reasons why people are reluctant to give honest feedback, including fear of reprisals or hurting our feelings, uncertainty about what to say, or not feeling qualified to give an opinion. As if these weren't barriers enough, there is also the possibility that your teammates may be jealous of your work or too invested in the outcome of your ideas to be objective.

In spite of these obstacles, there are some things you can do to encourage quality feedback from your team:

- Seek feedback widely—consider broadening the cross section of people whose feedback you request. Most of us have blind spots—people we just don't think of approaching for feedback. Perhaps there are support staff, clients, or individuals outside your team who can offer you a fresh perspective.

- Give a compelling rationale—let people know why you need their feedback and how it could be helpful to you, and possibly to them. You might tell your teammates: *"If this presentation goes poorly, I'm afraid we'll all find ourselves swimming upstream with this client. I really need your suggestions about how to perk it up."*

- Structure the feedback you want—be specific about the kind of feedback that will be helpful and make it easy for others to give. Instead of asking: *"What did you think of my presentation?"* you might ask: *"I'm afraid this presentation is running too long. Where would you suggest I might cut it?"* Consider developing a brief feedback checklist or questionnaire to distribute or email to your teammates, giving them a deadline to complete and return it.

- Finally, if some of the feedback you receive seems off the wall, thank the person anyway and don't dismiss his or her feedback completely. Sift through it for any nuggets of truth worth salvaging.

Situation 3

"One of my direct reports just won't open up and share opinions, even when I ask. Her favorite response is 'I don't know.' Her work is good, so I know she's not stupid. How can I get more input from her?"

The common mistake is to repeat variations of the question that already didn't work. A better approach is to use less threatening follow-up questions and approaches that elicit kernels of response, then build on them.

When your direct report says "I don't know," try coming back with questions that are more focused and specific, such as:

- *"Well, if you were to hazard a guess, which part of the proposal sounds best to you?"*

- *"What do you think is making it hard for you to give an opinion on this?"*

- *"How did you feel about the last part of the presentation?"*

An even more basic question to start with could be a direct one that only requires her to answer yes or no (*"Did that opening work for you?"*). Remember, your initial goal is to get her started and to be able to thank her for sharing something.

Some variations on the follow-up question include offering perspectives, rationales, and structure as ways to elicit feedback:

- *Perspective*—share your point of view before asking hers (*"I thought our data could have been stronger. What do you think?"*). This signals her that you are open to constructive criticism.

- *Rationale*—give a genuine and compelling reason why you want her input (*"I've been writing this report so long that I've lost perspective. Your fresh vision could be invaluable to me at this point."*).

- *Structure*—make it easier to share input by offering checklists or by emailing questions. Instead of putting the person on the spot, give her time to gather her thoughts and get back to you.

Reinforce any feedback you do receive by thanking the person and letting her know exactly how the feedback was helpful to you.

How to Encourage Constructive Feedback from Others: Participant's Workbook

Notes

Notes

Notes

Notes